Essays on Capitalism & The U.S. Economy
By : Hendrith Smith

Copyright 2014, Essays on Capitalism & The U.S. Economy by Hendrith Smith

All Rights Reserved by way of the United States Copyright Office

Printed and Produced in The United States of America.
First Published December 2014.

ISBN-13: 978-1986730303

Foreword:

This book series is a collection of essays that I have written and published mainly for other outlets such as LinkedIn and various newspapers and magazines. The book will be re-published with a new edition each year consisting of new essays/articles I have written since the last published edition.

"The Altruism of Capitalism"

Capitalism, yes, Capitalism - is Altruistic [Good]. And it requires a certain Altruism of each of us - "a selfless concern for the wellbeing of others." To understand this, I need to first describe the relationship between the broader system, and it's specific nodes. Essentially, we have Capitalism, Businesses, Families and individual People. Let's begin with Business. Business is about creating value for a specific group of people. Whether it's a Bakery, a Bank, a Textbook Manufacturer, or a platform like LinkedIn. For each business, Revenue and Profits come according to the extent of that it has created value for others. Profit is the reward a business gets when it serves others exceptionally well with it's value creation. And individual People within their family units, are the catalysts for this ongoing process. Capitalism is the broader system that allows businesses to be born and to function and thrive, and families and individuals to steward the monetary gain resulting from that. I think its time to re-romanticize Capitalism. Especially American Capitalism, which is supercharged and morally refined due to it's pairing with Democracy. But Capitalism has gotten a bit of a bad reputation as of the last several years. It's downright hated in some crowds. Many people have somehow learned to blame it for every Financial Crisis, Scheme, and

Business failure that occurs in our economy - and even for the existence of poverty and injustice. But Capitalism is the solution to these things, not the cause. Poverty has always existed, and Capitalism has lifted more people out of it than anything else has. Injustice has a long history, but only Capitalism makes it beneficial to a person to care more about a person's skills and character than what group they identify with. Financial crises come and go as sure as Winter precedes Spring - regardless of the economic system in reference. Blaming Capitalism would be like blaming Winter on the Snow Plows. Truth is, Capitalism makes it such that even in our Crises, we are more prosperous than nations who don't have Capitalism + Democracy, like we do. Its the cure. The remedy. The way - economically speaking.

See, I'm a student of the late Milton Friedman. And he taught a simple yet profound truth. Capitalism is the only system whereby the only way to self-serve is to serve others. In this system, the only way to help yourself, is to help a group of others, namely customers. In effect, Capitalism is the only system that requires of each citizen a certain level of Altruism, channels that Altruism into a collective mutual benefit, and rewards each citizen with money, according to the Altruism (Value Creation) they produce. There's an old term for situations like this, and it's called a "Win-Win." We all win, thanks to #thealtruismofcapitalism

Hendrith Smith

Banker, Financial Advisor, Author of 'The Wealth Reference Guide'

© 2017 Hendrith Smith. All Rights Reserved.

"Investment: An Engine of Equity"

What exactly is an Investment? Both the informed and the uninformed may be surprised to know that it isn't as complicated as it seems. Essentially, an investment is a purchase of ownership in something that is expected to increase in value during the term of ownership. Whether the Currency is Time, Love or Money; and whether the Ownership is symbolized by a Bank account balance, a Stock Certificate, or something as intangible as Knowledge; we exchange the currency for an expected increase in value of the thing we own. We invest time in University expecting that the Degree earned will give us an increase of earning potential. We invest love in our family expecting that the love will increase our happiness and the happiness of our spouse and children. And we invest money into a business expecting that our partial ownership of that company will be worth more in the forseeable future than it is at the time of initial investment. I care a lot about people, and I believe in "being my brothers keeper" and caring for those in need. And while I think some inequality is necessary and good, I believe poverty is not. I envision a world where we all are prospering and succeeding in life, though in different ways and to varying degrees. I would like to suggest a new way of promoting equity in our Capitalist society - investing in others, and empowering them to invest in themselves, in the marketplace, and in others. And while donations and subsidies have their place, Investment may be a superior alternative.

In our Capitalist-Democratic society, while levels of access may vary, access in and of itself is spread pretty evenly across all socio-economic classes. A Millionaire certainly has greater access to ownership due to their higher purchasing power, but those of low income are just as able to invest as anyone else. A single share of General Motors currently sells for about

$45.00 and as long as you have a record of being financially responsible with whatever money you have, you can open an investment account. And while a single share doesn't amount to wealth, it is a step on a long ladder to Equity. With persistence and sacrifice, a single share can become 10 shares; 10 shares can become 100 shares; 100 shares can become 1000 shares; and so on. We often think of Policy as the great engine of equity - "if only this Bill or this Law would pass." "If only that Legislation would be removed...." While Civic Engagement is Vital to the success of our Democracy, it may be time that we consider Investment the Great Equity Engine of our time - both investing in others and empowering them to invest. Maybe its time we stop trying to give the poor temporary fixes to their poverty, and instead empower them with the tools they need to build themselves up as we have by investing in them and empowering them to invest. This would be a Win-Win scenario where both sides would see a good ROI given both sides are financially responsible and steward the investment wisely. Milton Friedman said it best, "There is no such thing as a free lunch." And giving people a free lunch in the name of equality or equity is counterproductive. Wouldn't it make more sense to invest in them - and to help them invest in themselves and in others - to help them build a kitchen and stock their pantry that they may cook their own lunch instead of begging for it, and that they may then be to another as we were to them - an investor. Sometimes love, must be hard love. Hard things often take more time and effort to build, but provide more value.

Hendrith Smith

Banker, Financial Advisor, Author of 'The Wealth Reference Guide'

© 2017 Hendrith Smith. All Rights Reserved.

"Equity + Liberty > Equality"

"A society that puts **equality** before freedom will get neither. A society that puts freedom before **equality** will get a high degree of both." - Milton Friedman

It's time we as Americans collectively recognize the virtue of Capitalism. Many of us have come to be rather skeptical of it, some of us remain indifferent, while others scorn it. And then there are the rest of us, who seem in the minority today, who recognize the beauty and awesomeness of Capitalism and how it is a system that if applied correctly benefits all of us.

Capitalism is not some sort of "necessary evil," that by reason of our times, we have to endure for the sake of survival. Quite the opposite - Capitalism is a platform for all of us and each of us to receive value (money) in exchange for the value (service/products) we provide to other people or to a company. No other system rewards merit, hard work and creativity the way Capitalism does. No other system allows for so much growth and expansion. No other system has grace built into it - such that a man may be born poor and rise to great wealth; or, born wealthy, lose it all, and gain more back again - all according to value provided. We are not all "equal" - we all have unique strengths and weaknesses and stories. And it's much better to be equitable and allow each person to contribute value according to their uniqueness than to pretend we are all the same and thus limit the potential plethora of outcomes.

Equity is about everyone having access to the same opportunity to provide maximum value in their own unique way. It's different from equality, which seeks to ensure equal outcomes. Ensuring equal outcomes is not only bad, but immoral. What good is a one mile race if the referee from the beginning said that regardless of who actually crosses the finish line first, everyone will be considered first place or last place. Over time you would end up with a rather complacent group of runners who had no reason to improve their times, if they even attempted the run at all. We want a system where everyone, regardless of color, age, profession, or anything else, has the opportunity to achieve great wealth and success - and that is called Equity. We want a system where everyone may choose their own lifestyle andd design their life according to their desire - and that is called Liberty. And as a Banker, I would like to prospose an interesting idea - Equity + Liberty > Equality.

Hendrith Smith

"The Evolving Role of the Branch Bank"

The evolving role of the branch bank will be an interesting thing to witness. Right now, scores of people are talking about how hundreds of branches are closing all across the nation because statistically people are going to the branch less often and they are using digital banking more frequently and more holistically. Those scores of people are right, and wrong.

Digital banking will continue to play a pivotal role in retail banking. We will see greater technological advances that allow clients to manage their money online by themselves. But the need for a physical space dedicated to financial wellbeing is no more in threat of extinction than the need for a physical space to heal the sick. Advances in medicine have not eliminated the hospital, they have allowed for more creative ways to help people achieve health and avoid sickness. Advances in Digital banking will not eliminate the branch, the will allow for more creative ways to help people achieve financial well-being. Also consider this; just as the socio-political landscape is continually changing, the financial-economic landscape is also continually changing.

Clients will always and forever-more need financial experts to help them navigate and effectively capitalize on the present financial-economic reality. Just as well as we will always need lawyers to help us navigate and capitalize on the present socio-political reality, and teachers to help us adapt to new demands on knowledge and skills.

The transactional role of the bank is what will almost disappear. The bank will be a place for helping people achieve financial well-being - where clients and Bankers have thorough conversations and Bankers provide in-depth solutions to help people make, save and grow money.

I see branches coming back full circle to a new place of significance in the life of the people in the community. Branch Bankers will begin to take on more advisory roles with increased capacity to fulfill tasks that they once would have referred to a specialist on the insurance or investment teams, or to the back office. 10 years from now, when a client visits the branch, it will not be to conduct transactions as it was 10 years ago. Instead, they will visit the branch to sit with and receive financial consultation from a Banker - to help them structure their finances for tax efficiency, to help them capitalize on new financial sector laws and adapt to expired ones. Bankers 10 years from now will be series 6 and 7 licensed, Insurance licensed, and more. They will be able to place trades for clients and give investment advise, manage portfolios, assist with insurance claims and more.

The branch bank used to be one of the centers of American life. I'm bold enough to predict that it will be again.

Hendrith Smith

Banker, Financial Advisor, Author of 'The Wealth Reference Guide'

© 2017 Hendrith Smith. All Rights Reserved.

"The Altruism of Capitalism"

Capitalism, yes, Capitalism - is Altruistic [Good]. And it requires a certain Altruism of each of us - "a selfless concern for the wellbeing of others." To understand this, I need to first describe the relationship between the broader system, and it's specific nodes. Essentially, we have Capitalism, Businesses, Families and individual People. Let's begin with Business. Business is about creating value for a specific group of people. Whether it's a Bakery, a Bank, a Textbook Manufacturer, or a platform like LinkedIn. For each business, Revenue and Profits come according to the extent of that it has created value for others. Profit is the reward a business gets when it serves others exceptionally well with it's value creation. And individual People within their family units, are the catalysts for this ongoing process. Capitalism is the broader system that allows businesses to be born and to function and thrive, and families and individuals to steward the monetary gain resulting from that. I think its time to re-romanticize Capitalism. Especially American Capitalism, which is supercharged and morally refined due to it's pairing with Democracy. But Capitalism has gotten a bit of a bad reputation as of the last several years. It's downright hated in some crowds. Many people have somehow learned to blame it for every Financial Crisis, Scheme, and Business failure that occurs in our economy - and even for the existence of poverty and injustice. But Capitalism is the solution to these things, not the cause. Poverty has always existed, and Capitalism has lifted more people out of it than anything else has. Injustice has a long history, but only Capitalism makes it beneficial to a person to care more about a person's skills and character than what group they identify with. Financial crises come and go as sure as Winter precedes Spring - regardless of the economic system in reference. Blaming Capitalism would be like blaming Winter on the Snow Plows. Truth is, Capitalism makes it such that even in our Crises, we are more prosperous than nations who don't have Capitalism + Democracy, like we do. Its the cure. The remedy. The way - economically speaking.

See, I'm a student of the late Milton Friedman. And he taught a simple yet profound truth. Capitalism is the only system whereby the only way to self-serve is to serve others. In this system, the only way to help yourself, is to help a group of others, namely customers. In effect, Capitalism is the only system that requires of each citizen a certain level of Altruism, channels that Altruism into a collective mutual benefit, and rewards each citizen with money, according to the Altruism (Value Creation) they produce. There's an old term for situations like this, and it's called a "Win-Win." We all win, thanks to #thealtruismofcapitalism

Hendrith Smith
Banker, Financial Advisor, Author of 'The Wealth Reference Guide'
© *2017 Hendrith Smith. All Rights Reserved.*

"Investment: An Engine of Equity"

What exactly is an Investment? Both the informed and the uninformed may be surprised to know that it isn't as complicated as it seems. Essentially, an investment is a purchase of ownership in something that is expected to increase in value during the term of ownership. Whether the Currency is Time, Love or Money; and whether the Ownership is symbolized by a Bank account balance, a Stock Certificate, or something as intangible as Knowledge; we exchange the currency for an expected increase in value of the thing we own. We invest time in University expecting that the Degree earned will give us an increase of earning potential. We invest love in our family expecting that the love will increase our happiness and the happiness of our spouse and children. And we invest money into a business expecting that our partial ownership of that company will be worth more in the forseeable future than it is at the time of initial investment. I care a lot about people, and I believe in "being my brothers keeper" and caring for those in need. And while I think some inequality is necessary and good, I believe poverty is not. I envision a world where we all are prospering and succeeding in life, though in different ways and to varying degrees. I would like to suggest a new way of promoting equity in our Capitalist society - investing in others, and empowering them to invest in themselves, in the marketplace, and in others. And while donations and subsidies have their place, Investment may be a superior alternative.

In our Capitalist-Democratic society, while levels of access may vary, access in and of itself is spread pretty evenly across all socio-economic classes. A Millionaire certainly has greater access to ownership due to their higher purchasing power, but those of low income are just as able to invest as anyone else. A single share of General Motors currently sells for about $45.00 and as long as you have a record of being financially responsible with whatever money you have, you can open an investment account. And while a single share doesn't amount to wealth, it is a step on a long ladder to Equity. With persistence and sacrifice, a single share can become 10 shares; 10 shares can become 100 shares; 100 shares can become 1000 shares; and so on. We often think of Policy as the great engine of equity - "if only this Bill or this Law would pass." "If only that Legislation would be removed...." While Civic Engagement is Vital to the success of our Democracy, it may be time that we consider Investment the Great Equity Engine of our time - both investing in others and empowering them to invest. Maybe its time we stop trying to give the poor temporary fixes to their poverty, and instead empower them with the tools they need to build themselves up as we have by investing in them and empowering them to invest. This would be a Win-Win scenario where both sides would see a good ROI given both sides are financially responsible and steward the investment wisely. Milton Friedman said it best, "There is no such thing as a free lunch." And giving people a free lunch in the name of equality or equity is counterproductive. Wouldn't it make more sense to invest in them - and to help them invest in themselves and in others - to help them build a kitchen and stock their pantry that they may cook their own lunch instead of begging for it, and that they may then be to another as we were to them - an investor. Sometimes love, must be hard love. Hard things often take more time and effort to build, but provide more value.

Hendrith Smith
Banker, Financial Advisor, Author of 'The Wealth Reference Guide'
© 2017 Hendrith Smith. All Rights Reserved.

"Equity + Liberty > Equality"

"A society that puts **equality** before freedom will get neither. A society that puts freedom before **equality** will get a high degree of both." - Milton Friedman

It's time we as Americans collectively recognize the virtue of Capitalism. Many of us have come to be rather skeptical of it, some of us remain indifferent, while others scorn it. And then there are the rest of us, who seem in the minority today, who recognize the beauty and awesomeness of Capitalism and how it is a system that if applied correctly benefits all of us. Capitalism is not some sort of "necessary evil," that by reason of our times, we have to endure for the sake of survival. Quite the opposite - Capitalism is a platform for all of us and each of us to receive value (money) in exchange for the value (service/products) we provide to other people or to a company. No other system rewards merit, hard work and creativity the way Capitalism does. No other system allows for so much growth and expansion. No other system has grace built into it - such that a man may be born poor and rise to great wealth; or, born wealthy, lose it all, and gain more back again - all according to value provided. We are not all "equal" - we all have unique strengths and weaknesses and stories. And it's much better to be equitable and allow each person to contribute value according to their uniqueness than to pretend we are all the same and thus limit the potential plethora of outcomes.

Equity is about everyone having access to the same opportunity to provide maximum value in their own unique way. It's different from equality, which seeks to ensure equal outcomes. Ensuring equal outcomes is not only bad, but immoral. What good is a one mile race if the referee from the beginning said that regardless of who actually crosses the finish line first, everyone will be considered first place or last place. Over time you would end up with a rather complacent group of runners who had no reason to improve their times, if they even attempted the run at all. We want a system where everyone, regardless of color, age, profession, or anything else, has the opportunity to achieve great wealth and success - and that is called Equity. We want a system where everyone may choose their own lifestyle andd design their life according to their desire - and that is called Liberty. And as a Banker, I would like to prospose an interesting idea - Equity + Liberty > Equality.

Hendrith Smith

"The Evolving Role of the Branch Bank"

The evolving role of the branch bank will be an interesting thing to witness. Right now, scores of people are talking about how hundreds of branches are closing all across the nation because statistically people are going to the branch less often and they are using digital banking more frequently and more holistically. Those scores of people are right, and wrong.

Digital banking will continue to play a pivotal role in retail banking. We will see greater technological advances that allow clients to manage their money online by themselves. But the need for a physical space dedicated to financial wellbeing is no more in threat of extinction than the need for a physical space to heal the sick. Advances in medicine have not eliminated the hospital, they have allowed for more creative ways to help people achieve health and avoid sickness. Advances in Digital banking will not eliminate the branch, the will allow for more creative ways to help people achieve financial well-being. Also consider this; just as the socio-political landscape is continually changing, the financial-economic landscape is also continually changing. Clients will always and forever-more need financial experts to help them navigate and effectively capitalize on the present financial-economic reality. Just as well as we will always need lawyers to help us navigate and capitalize on the present socio-political reality, and teachers to help us adapt to new demands on knowledge and skills.

The transactional role of the bank is what will almost disappear. The bank will be a place for helping people achieve financial well-being - where clients and Bankers have thorough conversations and Bankers provide in-depth solutions to help people make, save and grow money.

I see branches coming back full circle to a new place of significance in the life of the people in the community. Branch Bankers will begin to take on more advisory roles with increased capacity to fulfill tasks that they once would have referred to a specialist on the insurance or investment teams, or to the back office. 10 years from now, when a client visits the branch, it will not be to conduct transactions as it was 10 years ago. Instead, they will visit the branch to sit with and receive financial consultation from a Banker - to help them structure their finances for tax efficiency, to help them capitalize on new financial sector laws and adapt to expired ones. Bankers 10 years from now will be series 6 and 7 licensed, Insurance licensed, and more. They will be able to place trades for clients and give investment advise, manage portfolios, assist with insurance claims and more.

The branch bank used to be one of the centers of American life. I'm bold enough to predict that it will be again.

www.ingramcontent.com/pod-product-compliance
Lightning Source LLC
Chambersburg PA
CBHW071002220526
45471CB00007B/3138